Franco Columbu

with DR. DICK TYLER

Weight Training and Bodybuilding

A COMPLETE GUIDE

FOR YOUNG ATHLETES

WANDERER

BOOKS

New York

To my sisters
Anna, Gonaria, and Celestina
To John Tyler

Photographs by Art Zeller, Jim Caruso, Albert Busek,
George Butler, and Anita Columbu

Published by Wanderer Books
A Simon & Schuster Division of
Gulf & Western Corporation
Simon & Schuster Building
1230 Avenue of the Americas
New York, New York 10020

Designed by Irving Perkins
Manufactured in the United States of America
7   8   9   10

Library of Congress Cataloging in Publication Data

Columbu, Franco.
  Weight training and bodybuilding.

  SUMMARY: Outlines beginning, intermediate, and
advanced weight training programs for those interested
in body building or merely in improving athletic skills.
  1. Bodybuilding—Juvenile literature.   2. Weight
lifting—Juvenile literature.   3 Physical fitness—
Juvenile literature.   [1. Weight lifting] I. Tyler,
Dick, joint author.   II. Title.
GV514.C64   646.7′5   79–10368

ISBN 0–671–33006–3

Contents

Weight Training and Bodybuilding

Introduction

The human body is the greatest instrument on the face of the earth. It is the original wonder. Every optic system ever devised is but a copy of your eyes. Every audio system was based on your ears. Bridges copy the interlocking facets of the spine. Hinges are based upon the joints of the body. The carburetor in the most sophisticated car can't compare with the grandeur of the internal organization of your body, and the computer hasn't been developed that approaches the potential of the human brain. There are virtually no limits to what you can do with your body, if it is properly trained and developed. I hope that this book will help.

In my own life, weight lifting and bodybuilding have been important from the moment I learned about them. I was born in Sardinia, a rugged island off the coast of Italy. And although my family was filled with strong, sturdy people, I was not a particularly sturdy child. In fact, I was rather skinny.

Nevertheless, I loved athletics, especially boxing. I entered the ring and won more than my share of fights. But still, I wasn't content. I couldn't seem to get the power I wanted behind my punches. I seemed to lack the snap needed for a knockout.

One day, while training in the gym, I noticed an athlete who was more muscular than any man I had ever seen. I watched him as he

Boxing in Italy

Dead lift—720 pounds

Benching 475 pounds

lifted weights. Finally, I had to ask him just how he had become so big and muscular. He answered with one word, "Weights."

I kept watching in fascination. He seemed to get bigger as he went along.

"But won't you get muscle-bound by doing all that weight lifting?" I asked.

He put down the weight he was working with. Wiping the sweat from his brow, he sat on one of the dumbbell racks and looked at the floor. I thought he hadn't heard me.

"Won't weights . . . ," I began again.

"Oh, I heard you," he interrupted. "I've heard that foolish question so often that I don't know whether to just say 'yes' or 'no' or give a lecture. Let me just say this. I wrestle, and until I took up weight training, I was losing. Now that I lift weights I'm stronger, faster, and better coordinated, *and* I'm winning my matches."

A few weeks later, I was in the gym alone. After working the speed bag for a while, I decided to work with some of the weights I had seen the wrestler use. It turned out to be more difficult than I had thought. I realized that I didn't know how to lift properly. And I didn't have the endurance to do any kind of high repetitions with the dumbbells or barbells. I reasoned that I would perform better in the ring if I increased my strength and my endurance. So I began lifting—with only the barest knowledge of what I was doing. In spite of this, my strength increased and my endurance improved so much that I won my last 19 fights with first or second round knockouts and was proclaimed the lightweight boxing champion of Italy. As my strength increased, I began to enter power-lifting contests. As my muscularity improved, I entered physique contents. I now hold world records in the middleweight class in power lifting: for the bench press, 485 pounds; for the squat, 650 pounds; for the deadlift, 750 pounds. I have also won—several times—every major physique title there is, including "Mr. Europe," "Mr. World," "Mr. Universe," and "Mr. Olympia."

I could have stopped there and rested on my laurels. But I was inspired by my wife, Dr. Anita Santangelo Columbu, and her consummate understanding of the physiology and mechanics of the human body. I wanted to learn more and do more. I went back to school, and after years of study, I became, like my wife, a chiropractic doctor. Now I bring to you my years of study and experience as an athlete, weight trainer, and doctor, with the desire that you may become a better athlete and a better human being.

11

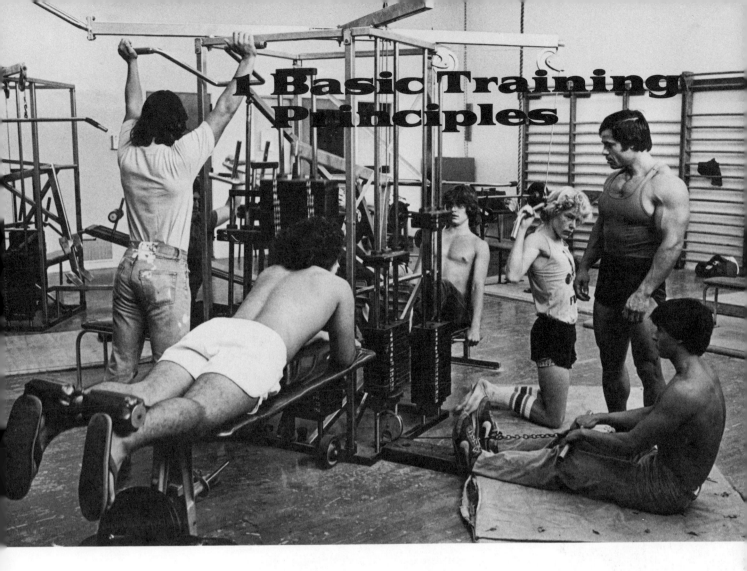

1 Basic Training Principles

Weight training can benefit everyone. It makes you stronger, tougher, and better able to perform in every kind of sport. This was understood in eastern Europe—where Olympic athletes have long been required to train with weights—long before it was understood here. It explains the fact that for years, athletes from eastern Europe won more medals—especially gold medals—than athletes from any other part of the world. But today the value of weight training is understood by serious athletes and coaches everywhere. And American men and women who want to be healthy and strong are discovering for themselves how much weight training can do. Even children as young as six can benefit. Of course, the weights children use must be very light (5-pound dumbbells and 20–25 pounds on the barbell). But still, the training provides a sound foundation and helps to set the young athlete on his or her way.

Weight training really can do wonders. But if you have never trained before, you must go slowly. Think of yourself as a child. You have all the equipment you need, but you must develop it in the right way. If you don't, it could be damaged before it gets a chance to blossom. You should be enthusiastic about your training, but not so enthusiastic that you injure the tissues you are trying to strengthen. Remember, before you can build a house, a foundation must be laid. The same thing is true when you are "building" a good body. The first goal of a training program must be the development of sound, all-round muscularity and strength. After that, you can narrow your focus and work in specific areas for specific strengths.

Whatever you do, you must learn to be instinctive in your training by "listening" to your body. It will tell you which programs you respond to best. This ability will come quickly if you are open to it—if you let yourself listen.

Many people have their muscles tested at some point in their training. I think it's a good idea. Chiropractic doctors, like myself, who are trained in Applied Kinesiology, can isolate and test specific muscles. When a weakness is discovered, reflex points are stimulated. This stimulation brings the muscle in question to its greatest strength. Since most muscles work together with others to achieve movement, you may do poorly at one exercise because (though you don't know it) one of your muscles is not doing its job. An examination will tell the tale. In fact, you really should have a complete physical checkup—one that includes a good neuromuscular-structural evaluation—before you begin serious training.

When you do begin to train, you must do some light warm-up exercises before each session. If you don't, you will strain and possibly injure your muscles. Be sure you know how to do each movement in the exercise correctly. Follow the instructions carefully. Ask for help or advice when you need it. Otherwise you won't get the benefit the exercise is designed to give.

Once you have the specific movement down, you can choose between two different styles of doing it. You may try to move only the muscles you are working on and keep the rest of your body still. Then your muscles will be more defined and they will gain a pleasing shape. Or you may lift in a looser or a "cheating" manner, and allow your whole body to help. This will enable you to lift heavier weights and your muscles will grow larger—although they will not have as much definition. As you become more advanced you will know the areas of your body in which you want greater size, those where power is more important, those where shape is more important, and those where you want size, power, and shape. You will be able to do your exercises accordingly.

Set aside a special time each day for training. Generally, the late afternoon, between four and six, is best. At that time, the body is warmed up, but not tired. Try never to miss more than one workout each week.

Don't train on either a full or an empty stomach. Eat something an hour or two before your workout. Wait at least a half hour after exercising before eating a meal.

Remember to keep your clothes comfortable while exercising. Smaller shirts make you look bigger and stronger, which is good psychologically.

The best way to achieve definite improvement is to set definite goals for yourself. Pick an important event: team tryout, a track meet, graduation, or your birthday, for example. Set a goal that you wish to achieve by the time that event comes around. (It shouldn't be too far into the future.) Having a specific goal and a specific time within which you want to achieve it will keep you training without becoming discouraged, and you will be less likely to miss workouts. Of course, your long-range goals should be to become an increasingly stronger athlete, and a healthier, sturdier, better-looking person.

All your exercises will be put in groups of repetitions called "sets." Sets are done with a pause between them. For example, if you did 10 repetitions and stopped for a minute's rest, those 10 repetitions would be a set. You might follow it with a second set, and then other sets that you feel are necessary. As you continue to exercise, the blood vessels in the exercised muscles expand or dilate to allow more fresh blood to get into the area of exercise. As a result of this "vascular engorgement," the muscles grow temporarily in what is called a "pump." It's a good bloated feeling. You know something is happening. After a while the pump goes away, but the good it did remains.

The training programs in this book are the result of several years of research. The amounts of sets and reps are different for each of the muscle groups, and the programs are designed to balance and strengthen the entire body so that you can perform better in every sport. Whatever your aims are, make the most of your training by following these important rules:

1. Select properly fitting training clothes and shoes, and keep them clean.
2. Never train without training shoes.
3. Keep your mind clear of problems and full of enthusiasm.
4. Never train when you are tired.
5. Always warm up properly.
6. Concentrate on each exercise. This will give you more strength.
7. Do not socialize between sets. Keep resting time between sets to a minimum.
8. Avoid all sugar or artificially sweetened products (food or drink, including honey) for at least two hours before beginning your workout and, of course, during the workout. Drink water or a small glass of natural juice. Do not drink any alcohol or any stimulant such as coffee.

9. Do each exercise according to the instructions in the book.
10. Visualize each muscle group growing while you exercise it.

All the exercise in the world isn't any good if you don't support your efforts with proper eating and sleeping habits. A later chapter will go into greater detail on specific nutritional concepts. But sleeping may be covered with some simple advice. First, you must sleep on a firm mattress that supports the contours of the body. Sleeping on your back with a pillow supporting the natural forward curve of your neck is best. Sleeping on your stomach tends to mechanically distort the body.

One more word of advice: While sleeping, dream of the future and the success you can make it.

2 Special Techniques, Information and Advice

Franco and Dick Tyler

PROPER BREATHING TECHNIQUES

We breathe, on the average, from 12–20 times per minute. We take each breath for granted. But we shouldn't. With each breath a miracle takes place.

When we breathe, oxygen comes in through the mouth and nose, goes into the trachea, on to the bronchi, to the smaller bronchioles, and finally into the alveolar, or air, sacs in the lungs. Here a miraculous transfer takes place. The oxygen that all cells need is exchanged for waste material (in the form of carbon dioxide) that the cells discard. The carbon dioxide is exhaled. And the oxygen is rushed to the cells that need it. Each time you breathe, this exchange of fuel for waste takes place. And as we said, you do this—on the average—12–20 times per minute.

When you exercise, the cells in your body have to work harder than "average." They burn up fuel faster. They produce waste material faster. You must breathe faster and more deeply in order to rush oxygen to the cells and pick up carbon dioxide.

You can see that good lung capacity is essential if you want your

19

body to work at peak efficiency. Breathing techniques—breathing in and out at the right time, the right rate, and in proper amounts—are just as important. Think of your body as a powerful ocean liner. The lungs are the furnace and oxygen is the coal. The more speed or power needed by the ship, the more coal must be fed into the furnace. If it isn't—at the right time and in the right amounts—the ship won't go. In the same way, you must "feed" your "furnace" properly, or you won't go.

When you are exercising, breathe deeply and inhale through the nose. Inhale during the relaxation phase of the movement and exhale during the exertion. I always think of inhaling as stoking the "furnace" for the strength that will be needed during the exertion. When I do my bench presses, for example, I inhale as the weight is lowered to my chest and exhale as I push the weight to arm's length. I inhale as I lower myself into a full squat position and exhale as I rise.

As you exercise, concentrate on developing the proper breathing rhythm. Work on it until it becomes a natural, not a labored, occurrence.

Like food, it is important that we get the right amount of oxygen, and that we get it when we need it. Never take for granted the kinds of food you eat—or the volume of oxygen you need. Pay attention to your body. Furnish what is needed when it is needed and you are bound to achieve dramatic and rapid progress.

THE GRIP

You can lift only as much as you can hold. That seems obvious, I know. But still, we shouldn't take it for granted. There are few things as important as the power in your hands. If your grip is secure, the muscles in the upper body seem to feel more power and, as a result, they respond more quickly.

Gripping strength has often been a mark of overall power. One famous strongman by the name of Vansaart was renowned for his ability to tear a tennis ball in half with his hands! An American strongman named Mac Batcheler astonished people by placing bottle caps between his fingers and bending them all at the same time. It is rumored that someone once hid a dime inside of the caps as a trick, and Mac bent it as well. And a strongman in Coney Island who understood the importance of a good grip made a lot of money by using it to cheat. He would bend over and lift a heavy dumbbell off the ground with one hand. Then, holding it, he would slowly return to a standing position. He challenged one and all to do the same. Professional and would-be strength athletes from all over the country tried. No one could do it. No one could even lift the weight clear of the floor. They couldn't get a good grip on it because the circumference of the shaft was so large.

One day, a professional strongman watched the performance. He wanted to accept the challenge. But he decided to do some investigating first. When the show was over, he went backstage. He saw that the Coney Island strongman's hands were not large; if anything, they were rather small. Then he examined the bar closely. He noted a small groove or notch in the shaft. Looking once again at the performer's hands, he noticed a ring on the lifting hand. He realized that a sharp edge on the ring might just fit into the groove, making the grip a little surer. Needless to say, he left without trying to lift the weight himself.

John Davis, the great American weight lifter, was another strongman who understood the importance of a good grip. Davis had relatively small hands, which wasn't too important when he was lifting an Olympic bar. One time, however, Davis accepted a challenge to lift the barbell used by Appollon, the French strongman. The barbell was actually an axle and wheels from a train. Appollon used it as a "show" lift. The weight was heavy, though not excessively. What made it so difficult to lift was the large circumference of the shaft and the fact that the wheels on either end were stationary so that there wasn't any rotation as the weight was lifted to the shoulders. This alone could almost tear the weight from the grip of a lifter. With considerable pressure, Davis attempted the lift and failed. He tried again. And again. Finally, he reversed the grip of one hand and got the bar off the floor. As the weight approached his shoulders, he switched back to a regular grip. From the shoulders he jerked it overhead for a successful lift. As soon as the weight was lowered to

21

the floor, Davis collapsed. He had lifted heavier weights in the past, but in this instance, the size of his hands prevented him from getting a good grip. It almost proved his undoing.

Remember these stories as you train. Work on your grip until it is as strong as it can be. Then work on it some more. Squeezing a rubber ball, doing wrist curls, reverse curls, and using a specially made gripping apparatus will help.

ON BECOMING MUSCLE-BOUND

A favorite myth—among lazy people—is that big muscles mean you're muscle-bound. The bigger the muscles, the more muscle-bound you must be. This myth has been around for a long time. And although most people today know better, it crops up again every once in awhile. When I was boxing, I trained with weights. The weight training increased my strength, endurance, stamina, and speed. I did not become muscle-bound. My flexibility and mobility were not decreased.

This doesn't mean that if you're big and muscular you'll never be muscle-bound. If you train improperly, you could get muscles that tie up easily. I was told of one young man who wanted big biceps more than anything. He did chin-ups as many times as he could, every day. And he did develop big, powerful biceps. But the biceps is the flexor muscle of the arm. He completely neglected his triceps, or extensor, muscle. As a result, he had arms that were unbalanced. It is said that he often woke up in the middle of the night in great pain, his arms cramped in a flexed position.

I don't know if this story is true, but it serves to illustrate the need to exercise for balance. If you train flexor and extensor muscles equally and well, you will not become muscle-bound. You will have a well-balanced, symmetrical and useful body.

YOUR HIDDEN SOURCES OF GREAT STRENGTH

Everyone is far stronger than he believes. We have a powerful animal inside us, and the right combination of stress factors brings him out. In physiology this is known as the "flight or fight mechanism." If someone were to stick a gun in your ribs and say, "Your money or your life," your heart would start beating faster, the pupils of your eyes would dilate, and your muscles would become like steel. All the body systems would be mobilized so that you could either run for your life or fight for it. This physiologic phenomenon is almost like a reflex.

Mental preparation

There are many stories of relatively weak people suddenly displaying great bursts of power. My favorite is the one about the young naval ensign during World War II. He was new in the Navy and his first assignment was to guard some very important papers—with his life, if necessary. The intense young man was determined to carry out his duties to the letter. He was assigned to a ship that was to take him and the documents he was guarding to a special rendezvous. For safekeeping, the papers were placed in a safe in the hold of the ship. The safe weighed about 350 pounds and was bolted to the deck.

One day, there was a practice alert. All personnel were to take their positions to abandon ship. Not realizing that it was just a practice alert, the young naval officer ran to get the papers from the safe. He had to fight his way past all the people going up the stairs. But he finally reached the safe. Then he realized that he didn't have the combination with him. He could hear the sirens blowing, and he envisioned the ship sinking, with all the vital papers on board. In panic, he struggled to open the safe. But he could not. Finally, he tore the safe from the deck, ripping the bolts as he did so. Hoisting the 350-pound hunk of metal on his shoulders, he made his way up the stairs to the top deck. Then he carried it to the ship bridge, where he placed it at the Captain's feet. When he was told that the alert had been just a drill, he collapsed and was in the hospital for weeks.

I myself have been turned on to great power by things that caused me stress. One such occasion was touched off by a well-known super heavyweight weight lifter. He had been interviewed by a local newspaper in connection with the National Championships being held in town. During the interview he said that bodybuilders were "mirror athletes" with overblown and relatively weak muscles. I was infuriated at reading such garbage. And for the next few days I couldn't think of anything but confronting the weight lifter. On the day of the meet, I got my chance. He came into the gym with a friend to look around. When I saw him, I ran over and challenged him to a contest of strength. He refused, saying that he wanted to save his strength for his lifting performance that night. His friend took up the challenge and I beat him handily at every contest we had. I was piling weights on bars from every place I could find a loose plate. I knew I could have beaten the super heavyweight that day—or for that matter, King Kong.

No one expects you to go on a sinking ship, or be insulted by strangers in order to increase your power. But you should realize the kind of potential you have inside you, and learn, through controlled desire, how to make it come out and work.

ESPECIALLY FOR BODYBUILDERS: POSING TIPS

A number of years ago, a well-known bodybuilder was winning almost all the local contests. He was considered a favorite to win the Mr. America contest. Only the immortal Steve Reeves had a chance of catching the young physique star. Then, so the story goes, at a very important meet prior to the Mr. America contest, he was called to the stage to pose. To everyone's surprise, he mounted the posing dais wearing a pair of tennis shoes, and chewing gum. He wasn't going to shock anyone. He had been caught off guard and, without thinking, ran from the dressing room to the stage. No one ever forgot that appearance. He never won another major event.

I realize that this example of improper posing is extreme. But it should help you understand how important a good presentation is. It's worth as much time and effort as you can give it. Remember, posing is not just a matter of flexing your muscles. Posing is an art.

I have seen all kinds of routines over the years. Some were so contrived and showy that they were comical. Others were so unimaginative that they were boring, even if the poser had a great physique. Start planning your routine now. If you work on it carefully, it can become a trademark of your physique.

The first thing to do is study your body in the mirror. Your eyes will probably be drawn to the things that please you the most. If you have good arms, you'll look for them. That's fine. You should learn to display those areas that you and your training partner or bodybuilding friends think are best. But you must also be aware of

your weaknesses. Most of us have them. And while it is important to display our good parts well, it is just as important to be able to discreetly obscure the weaker ones. The best example of someone who knew how to do both is the immortal John Grimek.

Grimek was to bodybuilding in the thirties and forties what Babe Ruth was to baseball or what John Unitas was to football. He was never defeated in a physique contest. He had incredible arms, legs and shoulders. But he also had some weak points. He lacked abdominal definition, had virtually no pectoral development and no muscular density in his back. An ordinary person might have gotten little more than prizes at local meets. Not so with Grimek. He was smart. He knew how to best subdue the faults while exploiting the grandeur of those body parts that were truly great. Instead of showing a "washboard" set of abdominals, he would demonstrate ab-

27

A winning posing routine

dominal control that left audiences gasping. After that he might display his incredible leg development. When he displayed a weak area, such as the back, he would give an amazing display of separating the scapulae, or shoulder blades. He made the audience aware of what he could do with what he had. By the time he was through with his routine, the crowd would be mad with excitement. Without a doubt, he was one of the great artists of the day.

Today, most bodybuilders realize the importance of good posing ability. Many bodybuilding contests even give awards for the "Best Poser," recognizing, as they should, the importance of the art of posing.

Observe the posing of others, but remember that a routine which looks good when I do it may not suit you. Study, practice posing in front of a mirror for at least ten minutes every day. Not only will you become better at it, but the posing itself will tend to define and separate the muscles for a more pleasing and finished appearance.

You must also practice putting on oil. The purpose of the oil is to accentuate muscular highlights. Unfortunately, too many people feel that the more oil they put on, the more highlights will be seen. They usually end up looking like they just stepped out of a bottle of cooking fat. Experiment with oil in front of the mirror. Don't use too much or too little. Ask other people for opinions.

An added feature of today's contests is music. Gone are the little bands that used to play some foolish dance music while the contestant was posing. These have been replaced by the wonders of stereo tapes with massive orchestrations of powerful themes from the classics and film scores. The overall effect has been inspiring to the audience and to the contestants as well. I myself have developed my posing routines around certain favorite themes that I feel complement my personality and my physique.

You must develop a routine that is yours. Find the music you like the best, the type you feel most inspired by. If possible, develop your routine around the music and bring a tape or a record of it with you when you go to a contest so that, if possible, it can be used.

If your routine is carefully worked out, it should be smooth, with no jerky movements whatsoever. No matter how good it is, however, it will suffer if the lighting isn't right. Before the contest, pose under the lights as they are set up. Have a friend observe in which positions the light best shows your physique, and then mentally, or with a marker or tape, mark the spot.

A good posing routine isn't just born; it must be personally developed. It can and should become the signature of your success—never a forgery.

MUSCLES, TENDONS, BONES, LIGAMENTS AND NERVES

Before we begin on your program, I think it would be a good idea to understand the equipment you'll be working with. Without making this a complicated anatomy lesson, let's examine just a few of the basic structures of the body and see how they work together to make you more effective.

Muscles

There are three basic types of muscle. Cardiac muscle for the heart, smooth muscle for organs such as the stomach and the intestines, and skeletal muscle to support and move the bones. It is skeletal muscle with which we shall be primarily concerned, but all types will benefit from constructive training. There are over 600 skeletal muscles, which means that muscles outnumber the bones they move by 3 to 1. This gives us great dexterity and sophistication in movement.

Tendons

Tendons are tough, fibrous bands at the ends of muscles. They attach muscles to bones and other structures. In the tendons are the "Golgi tendon apparatus," which send signals to the brain to indicate fatigue and stress. Often, the aching felt during strenuous exercise is being transmitted from the tendon, not the muscle. That is why it is important to include in your training program static, or isometric, exercises as well as full movement exercises.

Bones

There are 206 bones in the body. They form the skeleton, or framework, of the body. Muscles, attached to the bones by tendons, support the bones and move them from one position to another.

Ligaments

Ligaments are fibrous bands that bind bone to bone. Their tightness determines to a great extent the flexibility of the joints they serve. Care must be taken when you are engaging in a strenuous sport, because if a ligament is stretched too far, it can be permanently damaged. The joint it holds together will become "loose." This is one reason football players take so long to recover from knee injuries. When excessively stretched, the ligaments don't come back to their original length and you get a "trick knee." Exercise programs must be carefully paced so that the different parts of your body can be strengthened equally and without injury.

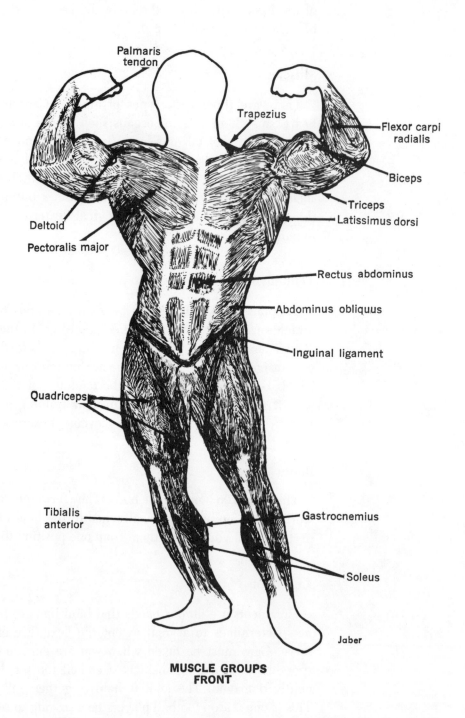

Palmaris
tendon

Trapezius

Flexor carpi
radialis

Biceps

Triceps

Latissimus dorsi

Deltoid

Pectoralis major

Rectus abdominus

Abdominus obliquus

Inguinal ligament

Quadriceps

Tibialis
anterior

Gastrocnemius

Soleus

Jaber

**MUSCLE GROUPS
FRONT**

34

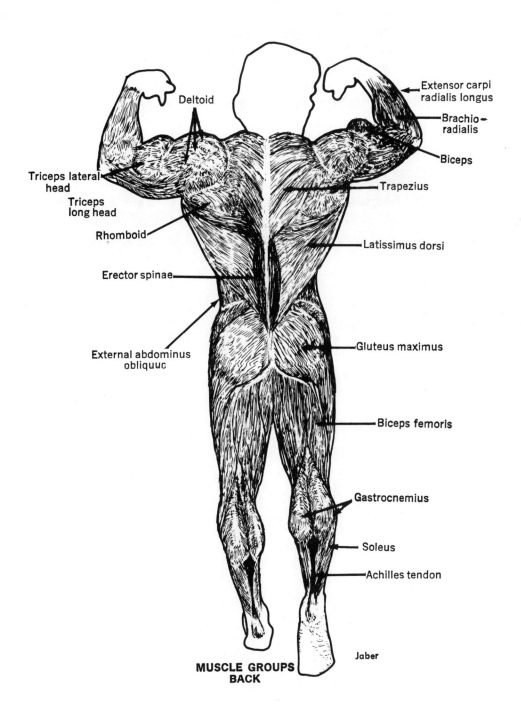

Deltoid

Extensor carpi
radialis longus

Brachio-
radialis

Biceps

Triceps lateral
head

Triceps
long head

Rhomboid

Trapezius

Latissimus dorsi

Erector spinae

External abdominus
obliquue

Gluteus maximus

Biceps femoris

Gastrocnemius

Soleus

Achilles tendon

Jaber

**MUSCLE GROUPS
BACK**

35

Nerves

The nervous system may seem irrelevant to the development of strength and size, but without nerves bones wouldn't move because muscles wouldn't flex. The nervous system has two major divisions —the central, consisting of the brain and spinal cord, and the peripheral, consisting of the nerves and ganglia outside of the brain and spinal cord. There are other divisions, too. But for us, the important thing to realize is that the nervous system is a vast network of "wires" that sends, receives and interprets signals from all parts of the body.

So there we have it. Nerves stimulate muscles which move bones through the tendinous attachments near joints that are held together by ligaments. Working together properly, you have the best machine ever conceived. To make it as strong as possible, place a (carefully programmed) increase in stress on the muscles, tendons and ligaments. In other words, lift heavy, become powerful.

3 Mental Discipline

I believe that the brain is the most powerful organ in your body. You can—and should—make it work for you. Without mental discipline, your physical performance will suffer. With it, you will excel. I don't know of any athlete—who's any good—who doesn't use his mind to back up and control his physical powers. There are no exceptions.

At a weight-lifting meet some years ago, I was watching the competitors prepare for their lifts. One rather small athlete really impressed me. Before each lift, he would stand stock still, face the bar squarely, place his hands on his hips and look up at the ceiling as if trying to gain some heavenly inspiration. Suddenly he would expel his breath and march up to the bar. He looked like he was going to bite it. He would stand directly over the weight and stare down at it contemptuously. Then he'd shake his head and arms and look down at the bar again. "No," he would say as he turned away. Then he would go to the chalk box just off the lifting platform and chalk his hands for a more secure grip. He would start his pacing all over again. It took almost fifteen minutes for him to make his attempt. But when he did, he was superb.

This is an extreme example, to be sure. But it points out a basic fact: Mental attitude is an extremely important part of any physical performance. Start working on it right now, as you train. If you want to excel, think in terms of "I will," not "I might." Don't accept the word "can't." Do it! Believe that you can—and nine times out of ten, you will be able to.

The most amazing example I know of the triumph of mental attitude concerns the French strongman, Appollon. He was 6′4″ and weighed 280 pounds. And he was just as strong as he looked. Appollon developed a strength act, the highlight of which was an "escape from jail." He was locked into a cage, and in order to get out, he had to bend the bars with his bare hands. The bars were made of iron, and he had new ones cast for each performance. In one town, the foundry made a mistake. The bars of the cage at Appollon's performance that night had been tempered into steel.

Not aware of the mistake, Appollon grasped the bars in his massive hands. He took a deep breath and hunched his shoulders. Then he began to exert his great strength on the bars. Nothing happened. He felt no give at all.

Appollon was puzzled. After all, he had done this same act for years without any trouble. True, some bars were harder to bend than others, but that just meant that he put out a little extra effort. Once again he tried to bend the bars. Once again, nothing happened.

It is said that Appollon was married to a very domineering woman who watched all his performances. Standing in the wings, she was convinced that her huge husband was just being lazy. She began to tap her foot with impatience—a sound Appollon had heard many times before. This spurred him into renewed action, but to no avail. The heavy bars remained straight.

Appollon never guessed that the bars were anything but the usual iron. So even now, there was not a thought of defeat in his mind. He just kept trying. Beads of perspiration began to form and his forearms throbbed with the engorgement of blood as he struggled to bend the steel. The audience began to murmur. When would the big strongman bend the bars? Then it happened. The bars began to bend, ever so slightly. Continuing the struggle, Appollon at last made an opening wide enough to squeeze through. He staggered off the stage and collapsed.

There is another example of the power of the mind that I myself saw happen some years ago. The man in question, a bodybuilder, used to come into the gym three times a week. Without removing his clothes, he would, like a ritual, walk over to the corner where an Olympic bar was loaded with 205 pounds. He would press it overhead once, then go to the locker room to change for his workout. Try as he might, he was never able to lift more than the 205 pounds on the bar. One day he came in, went over to the bar as usual, and lifted it as usual. But as he turned to go into the locker room, he glanced back at the bar. Something was different. He examined it closely. After a little figuring, he discovered that he had lifted 235 pounds—a full 30 pounds more than he had ever lifted in his life. Who knows, he might have been able to lift 50 pounds more. He had all that strength hidden under a lack of confidence!

Be aware of your attitude about your own strength and ability. Believe in yourself and in what you are trying to do. During your training sessions, keep the concept of achievement in mind. Think about what you will accomplish, not what you might accomplish. Give each exercise everything you've got. Concentrate so hard on the exercise you're doing that you become unaware of everything else. This kind of concentration is often aided by mirrors. That's why all good gyms are loaded with them. Look in the mirror while

39

you are exercising. Watch the muscle you're working on move, peak, and flex. You can almost see it grow.

Increase the power of your concentration, refuse to take "no" for an answer, and you will grow bigger, stronger and better at everything you try to achieve. Remember, mental discipline comes first; all else follows.

4 Beginning Training Program

Enthusiasm is wonderful. Without it, few things that we want would ever come to pass. As with everything, however, too much enthusiasm can be counterproductive. This is particularly true with exercising. So if you have never engaged in serious weight training before, be careful. The chances of injury are great—if a proper program isn't followed. I've seen many a young man come into the gym, inspired by a contest he saw the night before. He's just got to be like that "Mr. America." Because he's been getting results by doing three sets of each exercise, he figures that if he does six sets of each exercise, he should get twice the results. What he doesn't realize is that the exercise itself causes a breakdown in the tissue. The feeling of size is only temporary due to the engorgement of blood in the exercised area. It is when you're resting that the body repairs the muscle with such exuberance its tissue size increases. Too much exercise with too little rest doesn't allow a chance for sufficient repair. The result can be an actual diminution of size and an accompanying weakness. The body can be taught to accept increasing exercise requirements, but it must be carefully brought to that point.

The following is a training program I have designed for beginners. It will lay the foundation upon which you can build a championship body. If you have never trained before, do only one set of each of the exercises for one or two workouts. Then go to two sets, and finally the recommended number. The program should be done three times a week, with a day between each workout. Start with enough weight so that you can finish a complete set. As you get stronger and it becomes easier to lift the weights, increase the poundage and lower the reps a little and work up again. After a few months of this type of training, your body should be well-toned and you should be able to go on to the next, intermediate level of your training.

1. Warming Up

Each day, before you begin to exercise, you must take a few minutes to stretch your muscles. Stand with your feet about two feet apart and stretch your arms above your head, as if you were trying to reach the ceiling. Then bend over at the waist and, keeping your knees slightly bent, touch the floor. Do not force your muscles to stretch out. Take it slowly, and do as much as you can. About ten repetitions is best.

Another exercise I highly recommend before (and after) training is the cross-crawl. This exercise temporarily strengthens the muscles and helps keep them balanced. Stand and slowly raise your right arm and your left leg. Turn your head to the right as you do so. Return to your original position. Then raise your left arm and your right leg. Look straight ahead as you do so. Return to your original position and repeat. Do 2 sets of 25 reps.

2. Dead Lift   3 sets of 15 reps

A simple but very important exercise. Standing over a barbell, spread your hands to shoulder width and lower them to the bar. Grip the bar, one hand over, the other reversed on the shaft. This will allow a more secure hold (or, in bodybuilder's language, "purchase") on the weight. Keep your knees locked as you lift the bar off the floor and return to an erect position.

Dead lift

This exercise is particularly effective in developing the erector muscles on either side of the spine. These muscles are a "seat of power" because almost every standing or seated exercise, either directly or indirectly, involves the lower back.

3. Standing Press   4 sets of 15 reps

With your hands at shoulder width, grasp the barbell and raise it to your shoulders. Then raise (or "press") the bar over your head until your arms are fully extended.

This exercise is great for developing the shoulders, some of the muscles of the upper back and the extensor muscles of the arms.

Standing press

4. Squat or Deep Knee Bend   4 sets of 15 reps

Place a barbell on your shoulders, and then squat down to a full squat position. From this position, rise to a fully standing one.

This exercise develops the quadriceps muscle group at the front of the thighs. This group is the most powerful in the body and can take a lot of work. Not only will the exercise build great thigh size and power, but the heavy breathing which the movement requires will help pack on size and weight to the entire body. One word of caution: The heels should be placed on a small block of wood for better weight distribution. If you have a predisposition to lower back problems and you feel pain during the exercise, use a lighter weight or eliminate the exercise and do some leg movement, such as the leg press, instead. The leg press is done by placing the weight on your feet (usually done with a leg press machine) and extending your legs while lying on your back.

Squat

Barbell rowing

5. Barbell Rowing   3 sets of 12 reps

Bend over as if you were bowing to someone. Your upper body should be parallel to the floor. Lock your knees and place your hands on the shaft of a barbell, a shoulders' width apart. Pull the weight to your chest in repetitions.

This exercise works on the muscles of the back—particularly the latissimus dorsi which begins in the low back area and inserts into the upper arms. When well-developed, the "lats" give a winglike taper to the upper body which in turn makes the waist appear smaller for a pleasing visual effect.

6. Press behind the Neck
3 sets of 12 reps

This exercise is the same as the standing press, except that the weight is lowered behind the neck instead of to the front shoulders. It can be done in a standing or a sitting position. Either way, it increases the power and muscular definition of the upper back and shoulders.

Press behind the neck—start

Press behind the neck—up

Lateral raises

7. Lateral Raises   3 sets of 12 reps

You can stand or sit for this one, too. Grasp a dumbbell in each hand and raise your arms laterally until they are at shoulder height. Lower and repeat. For greater concentration, you can raise one arm at a time.

Lateral raises exercise the deltoids, powerful caps of muscle on the ends of the shoulders. When well-developed, they visually broaden the shoulders. From the standpoint of power, their development is imperative to all shoulder movements.

47

*Triceps extension
—start*

*Triceps extension
—up*

8. Triceps Extension   4 sets of 12 reps

Again, you can either stand or sit, whichever makes you feel more comfortable. Place your hands on the shaft of a barbell, about two hands width apart. Raise the bar above your head, then lower it behind your neck. Be sure to keep your upper arms close to the sides of your head. Only your elbows are bent. From the lowered position press the weight overhead by moving your forearms until your elbows are locked.

48

This movement exercises the triceps, the horseshoe-shaped muscle group at the back of the upper arm. While the biceps are the "show" muscle, the triceps take up almost two-thirds the muscular size of the arm when proportionately developed.

9. Dumbbell Curls 　　　　　　　　　3 sets of 12 reps

This exercise is done sitting or standing. Grasp a dumbbell in each hand. Brace the elbow of one hand and curl the weight to your shoulder. Lower, and repeat. Now do the same with the other hand.

This exercise is excellent for concentrating on muscular movement. Watch the muscle move as you work. You can almost see it grow.

Dumbbell curls

Leg raises

10. Leg Raises   **3 sets of 25 reps**

While lying on a bench, lock your knees and flex your thighs until they are at a right angle to your upper body. If at first you find it difficult to keep your knees locked, do the movement with your legs bent. Later, when you have more strength and endurance, try it again. When you are really advanced you can do these from the chinning bar.

Leg raises exercise the lower abdomen, the portion of the waist just below the navel. It is one of the most difficult areas to reach productively.

11. Sit-Ups   3 sets of 25 reps

With your knees bent (to prevent your thigh muscles from help-ing in the pull), and with your hands behind your neck, raise your upper body until your head touches your knees. This exercise is a good workout for the entire abdominal area.

Sit-ups

5 Intermediate Training Program

By the time you have worked on the beginning program for two or three months, you should feel little or no residual pain or muscle soreness from the exercises, and there should have been a substantial increase in your strength. You are ready for the intermediate training regimen, which aims at building a more solid muscularity. At times you will notice differences from the beginner's program in the number of sets and reps. In such cases you may have to vary the amount of weight you are using to accommodate these changes. The exercises which follow should be done three times a week with a day between each workout. The program may be used for up to six months with variations in weights and reps as you continue to improve in strength and endurance. You should be ready to really explode into the advanced program by the time you're done.

1. Seated Press behind the Neck   4 sets of 8 reps

Sit down, take a medium-wide grip on a barbell, and hold it at arm's length. Lower the bar to the base of your neck, inhaling as you do so. Then exhale as you quickly press it back to the starting position. Keep your back straight, braced if possible, throughout the exercise. Perform the reps in a continuous manner without pausing. It will be very helpful, particularly when you get to handling heavier poundages, if you can take the barbell from a squat rack, a power stand, or a special bench like the one in the exercise photos opposite.

This exercise is the best all-round deltoid developer there is. It works all three heads of the deltoid muscle, the lateral head getting the most benefit. It stimulates the entire shoulder girdle and even works the trapezius muscles a little.

2. Bench Press   **4 sets of 12 reps**

Lie flat on a bench, take a medium grip on a barbell and lower it until it just touches your chest. Then press it straight up, until your arms are fully extended.

The bench press is a great chest developer and the results can be enhanced with proper breathing. Inhale as the weight is lowered and exhale as you press. Watch your chest and your endurance grow.

Bench press
—start

Bench press
—down

Incline bench press

3. Incline Bench Press   **3 sets of 12 reps**

Lie on an inclined bench. Take a medium grip on the barbell, and lower it to the upper portion of your chest. Raise it to arm's length. Repeat. Breathing in while lowering, and out while pressing, can give better results.

This exercise affects the chest in a completely different way. Because the body is inclined, the upper portions of the pectoral, or chest muscles, are brought into play. This tends to give a higher appearance to the chest.

54

4. Lateral Raises   4 sets of 12 reps

This is the same exercise described in the beginning program. Now vary it by leaning forward during every other set. This will give an extra workout to the posterior portion of the deltoid muscle.

5. Front Raises   3 sets of 10 reps

While the blood is still pumped into the area from the lateral raises, it's a good idea to work the front portion of the shoulders. With a dumbbell in each hand, raise your arms one at a time until they are fully extended and parallel to the floor. Make sure that 10 reps are done for each arm.

Front raises

6. Upright Rowing   3 sets of 10 reps

While standing, take a narrow grip on a barbell and let it hang at arm's length in front. Now bring the weight up to your chin, lower it, repeat. This exercise is excellent for the deltoids and has an excellent effect upon the upper back, forearms and biceps.

Upright rowing

7. Chins behind the Neck   4 sets of 10 reps

Take a wide grip on a chinning bar. From a dead hang position, pull yourself up and under until the back of your neck touches the bar. Lower yourself and repeat.

Chinning is good exercise for the rhomboid muscles, the middle trapezius and the latissimus dorsi. The wide grip tends to isolate the scapulae, or shoulder blades, and pull them away from the midline of the body.

57

8. One-Arm Dumbbell Rowing   **4 sets of 10 reps**

Bend forward as if bowing from the waist. Grasp a dumbbell in one hand and support your weight with the other hand on a chair or bench. Do 10 reps with one hand then with the other.

This exercise allows you to isolate and work on one lat at a time.

One-arm dumbbell rowing

Triceps pushdown

9. Triceps Pushdowns   5 sets of 12 reps

I like this one a lot because it's a pretty restricted movement and I can really concentrate. A pulley such as a lat bar is needed. Hold your elbows at your sides and grip the bar, your hands close together, dorsal, or knuckle, side up. With your hands touching your chest for a starting point, press down until your elbows are locked. If done strictly, you'll feel a great rush of blood, of a "pumping" effect, before the third set.

59

Dumbbell curl

10. Dumbbell Curl   **4 sets of 10 reps**

With a dumbbell in each hand, lean back on an incline bench. Let the weights extend the arms to a natural hanging position. From there, curl the weight to your shoulders. Return to the original position. Repeat. Inclining the body isolates the movement for a more direct effect upon the biceps. There are many variations to this movement as there are for almost all movements. Here is one I like a lot: While doing the exercise, have someone (a partner) restrict the movement of your arms by applying a steady pressure on your elbows from behind. The effect is remarkable.

11. Lying Triceps Press   4 sets of 12 reps

Lie flat on a bench, take a close grip on a barbell, and extend it directly overhead. Without moving the upper arms, lower the weight to your forehead and extend immediately overhead again.

Lying triceps press

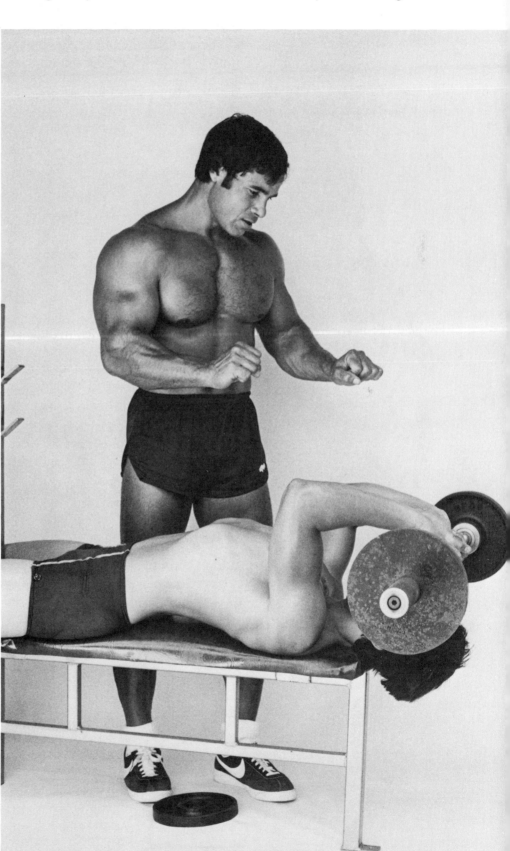

12. Preacher's Bench Barbell Curl   3 sets of 10 reps

A preacher's bench is a padded inclined surface over which you can drape your arms so that your upper arms are restricted. Standing in position at the bench, take a close grip on a barbell, extend your arms, then curl the weight to your shoulders. Bring the bar back to the original position. Repeat.

This exercise is another excellent way to work on your biceps. It isolates them, gives them the best possible shape, and adds to their size and power.

Preacher's bench barbell curl

Leg extensions

13. Leg Extensions   5 sets of 20 reps

This is done in a sitting position on a leg extension machine. Place the machine's bar across your ankles, then extend your legs until your lower legs are parallel to the floor. This exercise has an excellent effect on the lower portions of the quadriceps, or thigh, muscles.

14. Leg Curl   3 sets of 20 reps

Lie face down on a leg extension machine. Position the machine's bar across the back of your ankles. Curl the weights up, using the hamstring muscle groups (the semimembranosus, semitendinosus and biceps femoris muscles). When well-developed, these muscles give a "completed" fullness to the thighs. This exercise also benefits the calf muscles.

Leg curl

Squat

15. Squat   3 sets of 12 reps

This is the same exercise as in the beginning program. Fewer sets and reps are done because you'll be using more weight here and because there are other exercises in this program that affect the same muscle group.

65

Calf raises

16. Calf Raises   5 sets of 15 reps

Stand with your toes on a block. The block should be high enough to allow a full extension of the calf muscles. Lock your knees and flex your calves until your toes are pointed.

This exercise adds size and definition to the calves, which is essential if you want exceptional overall leg development.

17. Sit-Ups   **4 sets of 25 reps**

This is the same exercise as in the beginning program. More sets are done here.

18. Leg Raises   **4 sets of 30 reps**

This is the same exercise as in the beginning program. More reps are done here.

Beyond leg raises—the body raise

6 Advanced Training Program

By the time you reach this level of training, you have been working out for six months to a year. Your muscles should have shape, size and power. If you also developed good eating and sleeping habits along the way, you are probably healthier now than you have ever been in your life. You could stop here, continue the same exercises you've been doing and stay in good condition. That is admirable in itself. But the program which follows is for those of you who want to go further. The workouts are hard. They take motivation and dedication. But they could go a long way toward making you a champion.

THREE TIMES A WEEK   1. **Bench Press**   **6 sets of 10 reps**

This exercise is the same as in the intermediate program. But here you do more sets and reps. Remember that the pause between sets is just a break to give you a chance to regather your strength. It should never be longer than a minute or two, and it should never be used to socialize. Don't do anything that might make you lose your concentration.

Bench press

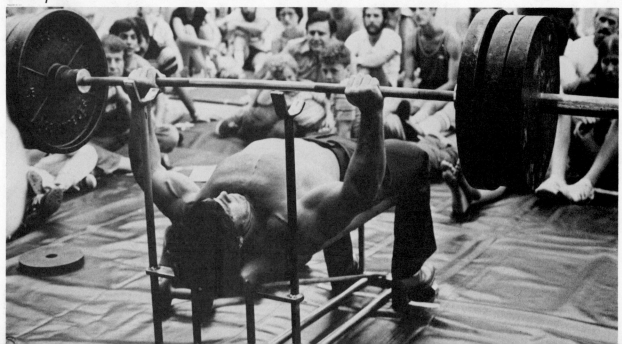

2. Incline Bench Press   4 sets of 10 reps

In the intermediate program, this exercise was done with a barbell. This time, I recommend dumbbells. By using a separate weight in each hand, you can lower the weights even more because of the loss of restriction from the bar on the chest. As a result, there is a greater stretching effect and more of the muscle can be reached. As the weights are pushed overhead, the dumbbells are brought together, which gives a cramping effect to the inner heads of the pectoral muscles.

3. Dips   3 sets of 10 reps

This exercise is done on parallel bars. Grip the bars, your elbows in a locked position. Lower your body as far as possible, then raise it until your elbows are in a locked position again.

This exercise is very good for the triceps, the chest and the shoulders. In fact, for all-round development of the upper body, this exercise is the best there is.

Dips

4. Chins behind the Neck   4 sets of 10 reps

This exercise is the same as in the intermediate program. You can make it more difficult, and therefore more effective, by strapping extra weights around your waist.

5. Chins in front of the Neck   4 sets of 10 reps

This is the same as exercise 4, except that you pull up to the front of your neck. This makes it a good exercise for the chest as well as the back.

Chins in front of the neck

Rowing

6. Rowing   4 sets of 10 reps

Here is a third variation of the rowing exercise. Load weights onto only one end of a barbell. Secure the other end. Clasp your hands around the weighted end of the barbell shaft, lift it to your chest, then lower it.

7. Press behind the Neck   4 sets of 10 reps

This is the same exercise as in the beginner's program.

8. Lateral Raises   4 sets of 10 reps

This is the same exercise as in the beginner's program.

9. Bent-Over Lateral Raises   4 sets of 10 reps

Do lateral raises, as in exercise 8, but bend forward at the waist as you do them. This will give strenuous exercise to the posterior portions of the deltoids and the muscles of the upper back.

Bent-over lateral raises

Triceps pushdowns

10. Triceps Pushdowns   6 sets of 10 reps

This is the same exercise as in the intermediate program. The bent-over lateral raises you just did have already stimulated muscle growth in the triceps. After you complete the pushdowns, the pumping effect will be marked. This will encourage more rapid muscular growth and power.

73

11. Dumbbell Curls   5 sets of 10 reps

You can do these curls just as you did them in the intermediate program. Or you can do a variation. There are as many variations as there are body types. And dumbbells, because of their lack of restriction, encourage a greater variety of movements than any other piece of exercise equipment. One of my favorite forms of dumbbell curling is alternating the regular curl with a Zottman variation.

George Zottman was an old-time strength athlete with a great pair of arms and a phenomenal gripping power. In the curl he developed, the movement is begun with your arms at your sides and the dorsal, or knuckle, side of the hand up. As you curl the weight up, rotate it evenly so that when it is at shoulder height, the palm surface of your hand faces your chest. As the weight is lowered, rotate your hand back to its original position. This exercise develops the biceps in a very different manner and literally pours blood and power into the forearms.

12. Lying Triceps Extensions   4 sets of 10 reps

Lie flat on a bench, the shaft of the barbell just touching your forehead. Extend the weight overhead until your arms are locked. Be sure to keep your upper arms perpendicular to your body while straightening your arms. If possible, a training partner might help with some restriction.

13. Preacher's Bench Barbell Curl   3 sets of 10 reps

This is the same exercise as in the intermediate program. If you don't have a preacher's bench, do the following exercise instead.

Standing Barbell Curls   1 set of 8 reps

This is a basic barbell movement which creates a tremendous amount of size and power in the biceps. I advise that it be done with as heavy a weight as possible. Start with your arms straight down. Curl the bar upward, keeping as close as possible to your shoulders. The upper body may move very slightly. Form is a real priority here. If you squeeze the bar, you may be able to do an extra rep or two.

Do not pause when you are finished with this exercise. Go on immediately to the next one.

*Lying triceps
extensions*

Standing barbell curls

Forearm wrist curl

14. Forearm Wrist Curl   3 sets of 10 reps

The forearms are a relatively small area when you consider all the muscles that are packed in there. For most people, the forearms and the calves are the most difficult areas to pack size onto. Of course, any exercise that requires gripping will benefit forearm size, but for maximum results, specifically designed movements are best. This one, the wrist curl, is excellent.

With your forearms lying on your thighs, your palms up and hanging over your knees, grasp a barbell with your fingers. Slowly curl the weight into the palm of your hand, and then flex the wrist as far as possible. Lower the weight and repeat. Concentrate by watching the forearms work, and you'll almost see them grow.

15. Reverse Wrist Curl   3 sets of 10 reps

Turn your forearms so that your palms face down. Again, grasp the bar and then flex the wrist as far back as possible. As with the previous exercise, concentrate and watch the muscles grow.

16. Pullovers   3 sets of 15 reps

Lie flat on a bench, your arms extended beyond your head and dropping toward the floor. With a narrow grip, grasp a barbell and pull it over your head to your chest. Lower and repeat. This is an excellent exercise for expanding the size of your chest and developing the lower portions of the pectoral, or chest, muscles. Breathing is exceptionally important here. Breathe in as the weight is lowered and exhale as it is brought to the chest.

17. Squat   4 sets of 10 reps

This is the same exercise as in the beginner's and intermediate training programs.

18. Leg Extension   5 sets of 20 reps

This is the same exercise as in the intermediate program.

19. Leg Curl   4 sets of 20 reps

This is the same exercise as in the intermediate program.

20. Calf Raises   5 sets of 20 reps

This is the same exercise as in the intermediate program. For a more complete calf development, vary the way you point your toes —in for one set, out for the next set, and so on.

Calf raises

21. Sit-Ups   5 sets of 30 reps

This is the same exercise as in the beginner's and intermediate training programs.

22. Leg Raises   5 sets of 30 reps

This is the same exercise as in the beginner's and intermediate training programs.

23. Side Bends   2 sets of 50 reps

While standing, grasp a dumbbell in one hand, lean as far as you comfortably can in the opposite direction from the weighted hand, then straighten up. Repeat 50 times. Change hands and do the opposite side. Rest for a moment and repeat. This exercise trims the waist and develops the obliquus externus muscles.

7 The Split Routine

A few weeks ago I was looking at some old films of bodybuilding contests held in the forties and early fifties. It was hard to believe what I saw. Some of the legendary bodybuilders were posing. A few of them were so famous that, to a bodybuilder such as myself, just their names conjured up thoughts of bodybuilding perfection. Yet, to my dismay, most of them probably couldn't win or even place in today's shows.

The same kind of thing is true in other areas of athletics. Not too long ago, the 4-minute mile was considered "unbeatable." It is certainly not unbeatable today. The 60-foot shotput was thought to be the "ultimate distance" that man could achieve. No longer. Why? What has happened to account for these radical changes in standards? Why do we demand more from athletes today? Why do we get more? One major factor, especially in bodybuilding, is the marked improvement in training programs. For years, the standard program consisted of 3 sets of 10 reps of each exercise 3 times a week. Good results were obtained, but only to the potential of the exercise, not to the potential of the individual doing the exercise. But at some point, individual bodybuilders began to experiment. They began to train more often than 3 times a week. They did more than the standard number of sets and reps. And they got results. Muscularity improved. Strength improved. And standards went higher and higher.

As the competition in major physique and strength events became more intense, competitors found it necessary to train longer and harder than ever. But there were two problems. In the first place, most of them had jobs. They couldn't give all their time to training. Secondly, long, strenuous training sessions sometimes caused more tissue breakdown than buildup. The body needed a rest. It needed time between workouts if it was to increase in size and strength. The solution to both problems was a program called the "split routine." This program allows the advanced athlete to concentrate on heavy exercises. But it is structured so that the body has time to recuperate in one physical area while another is being trained. And it leaves the bodybuilder enough time to hold a job.

The following split routine is one that worked well for me. You should use it only as a guide. It may not be the perfect one for you. You may wish to do exercises other than the ones I chose. You may need different sets and reps, or perhaps a regrouping of the exercises. In other words, here as in all programs, train instinctively. Do what you feel you respond to best.

Before this, you were training 3 times a week. Now, if you're ready, try 6 times a week and watch the results. I don't, however, recommend continuous use of this kind of program. It is best used for about 3 months at a stretch, perhaps the last 3 months before a contest, in order to put on some finishing touches. And, except for contest conditioning, skip a workout every so often. Listen to your body. If it says it's too tired, let it rest. Assuming that all is well—that you feel stronger than ever and that you want to reach the highest level you possibly can, this kind of program is for you.

MONDAY—WEDNESDAY—FRIDAY

CHEST

1. Bench Press   **5 sets of 8 reps**

This is the same exercise described in earlier programs.

2. Incline Bench Press   **4 sets of 8 reps**

This is the same exercise described in earlier programs. Do it with either dumbbells or a barbell.

3. Dips   **4 sets of 10 reps**

Dips were described in the advanced training program. They can be made more difficult—and therefore more effective—if you tie weight around your waist.

4. Flies   **3 sets of 10 reps**

Lie on your back on a bench with a dumbbell in each hand. Extend your arms straight up and turn them so that your hands face one another. Take a deep breath, as you lower the weights to shoulder height. Exhale as you bring your arms back to the starting position. This is a great exercise for expanding the rib cage and developing the inner heads of the pectoral muscles.

Dips

80

SHOULDERS

5. Press behind the Neck   4 sets of 10 reps

This is the same exercise described in earlier programs.

6. Lateral Raises   4 sets of 10 reps

This is the same exercise described earlier. You can vary it by using one arm at a time or by standing laterally to a pulley machine and doing raises with the pulley.

7. Bent-Over Lateral Raises   4 sets of 10 reps

This is the same exercise described in earlier programs.

8. Front Raises   2 sets of 10 reps

Stand with a dumbbell in each hand, your knuckles forward. Raise one weight at a time to shoulder height. Return to the starting position. Remember: It's 10 reps with each hand. The frontal portions of the deltoids are really worked with this exercise.

9. Pullovers   4 sets of 15 reps

This is the same exercise described earlier. An excellent variation is to cup your hands under one end of a dumbbell. Then do the pullover just as if you were using a barbell.

Pullovers

LEGS AND CALVES

10. Squat   **6 sets of 8 reps**

This is the same exercise described in earlier programs.

11. Leg Extensions   **6 sets of 15 reps**

This is the same exercise described in earlier programs.

12. Leg Curl   **4 sets of 15 reps**

This is the same exercise described in earlier programs.

13. Calf Raises   **10 sets of 20 reps**

While this is the same exercise described earlier, you'll note that here there is a marked increase in the number of sets. This is because it usually takes a great deal of work to reach the muscles of the calves. The gastrocnemius and soleus muscles make up the bulk of the calf area and are the muscles that propel you forward when you walk. Since we all walk, the calves get a great deal of work. To make the calf muscles grow, therefore, you must give them an extraordinary amount of work.

14. Sit-Ups—Leg Raises—Side Bends   4 sets of 30 reps

These exercises are combined. Do 30 sit-ups, followed immediately by 30 leg raises, followed immediately by 30 side bends. Rest and then do the second set.

TUESDAY—THURSDAY—SATURDAY   LATS

1. Chins behind the Neck   **4 sets of 12 reps**

Same exercise as described in earlier programs.

2. Chins in front of the Neck   **4 sets of 12 reps**

Same exercise as described in earlier programs.

Chins

3. Rowing

4 sets of 12 reps

This is the same exercise as described in earlier programs. It can be done to good effect with either dumbbells or a barbell.

4. Pulley Rowing

3 sets of 10 reps

This is one of my favorite lat exercises. With the right amount of weight, you can literally feel the stretch of the muscles in extension. While seated on the floor, take a close grip on the pulley handles and pull them to the lower margin of your chest.

Pulley rowing

ARMS

5. **Triceps Pushdowns**   6 sets of 10 reps

Same exercise as described in earlier programs.

6. **Dumbbell Curl (Zottman)**   5 sets of 12 reps

Same exercise as described in earlier programs.

7. **Lying Triceps Extension**   4 sets of 12 reps

Same exercise as described in earlier programs.

8. **Preacher's Bench Barbell Curl**   4 sets of 12 reps

Same exercise as described earlier.

*Preacher's bench
barbell curl*

Narrow-grip bench press

9. Narrow-Grip Bench Press   4 sets of 10 reps

This is the same as a wide-grip bench press, except that the hands are about 6″–8″ apart. Doing it this way not only develops the inner heads of the pectoral muscles but has a great effect upon the triceps.

10. Concentration Curl   8 sets of 10 reps

Sit on a bench with your elbow and the weight braced on your thigh. Curl the weight to your shoulder. Do this slowly and watch your biceps while you work. Think power, size and shape all the way.

11. Wrist Curl   3 sets of 15 reps

Same exercise as described earlier.

12. Reverse Wrist Curl   3 sets of 15 reps

Same exercise as described earlier.

13. Calf Raises   5 sets of 25 reps

Same exercise as described earlier.

14. Sit-Ups—Leg Raises—Side Bends

Same combination of exercises as described earlier.

One day a week, practice the dead lift as described in the first training program. Beginning with a relatively light weight, do 2 sets of 10 reps. Increase the weight and do 1 set of 6 reps. Increase the

Concentration curl

weight again, and do 1 set of 4 reps. Increase it again and do 2 reps. Finally, increase the weight to the maximum you can hold and do 1 rep. This will help keep tone and strength in the erector muscles of the lower back, so important to the strength of the entire body. If doing the exercise causes pain or discomfort, see a chiropractic doctor.

If you can do the split routine honestly and completely, you have reached a plateau of physical maturity and emotional maturity as well. It takes a good measure of persistence, motivation, endurance and strength. Congratulations—nothing can stop you now.

8 Training for Sports

In the past, coaches and trainers prescribed every kind of exercise they could think of to help their athletes get stronger and better at their sport. But they stayed away from weight-training exercises. They accepted the then common prejudice against the use of weights, and assumed that big muscles mean you can't move quickly or well. Today, they know better. We all do. In fact, I can't think of any great athlete, professional or amateur, who hasn't achieved some measure of that greatness through weight training. And I can't imagine a coach who doesn't understand that weight-resistance exercises, properly tailored for a particular sport, are the best way to increase coordination, strength and endurance. We've come a long way.

What follows is a series of weight-training programs designed to suit specific sports. They don't have to be followed to the letter. It would be best if you yourself carefully analyzed your sport and the weaknesses you have and train accordingly. Be specific for specific results. For example, if you play basketball and you'd like to get more height into your jump, concentrate on thigh and calf work. If you're a swimmer, and you want to have more power in your pull, copy the moves you do in swimming—with weights. Rowing exercises and pullovers would be especially helpful. In other words, be aware of your weaknesses and tailor your exercises to overcome them. As I've said many times, become instinctive in your training. Your body has a special language. Listen to it.

You should not take part in any other weight program while you are doing one of these. Follow the program of your choice three times a week—and watch the results.

FOOTBALL, BASEBALL, TENNIS, RACQUETBALL

The exercises in this program concentrate on leg, shoulder, and wrist work.

1. **Bent-Over Lateral Raises**	3 sets of 15 reps
2. **Lateral Raises**	3 sets of 15 reps

3. Front Raises	2 sets of 15 reps
4. Lying Triceps Press	3 sets of 15 reps
5. Wrist Curl	3 sets of 10 reps
6. Reverse Wrist Curl	3 sets of 10 reps
7. Leg Extension	3 sets of 10 reps
8. Calf Raises	4 sets of 15 reps
9. Running	

This doesn't mean "jogging," which I consider detrimental to most people's structure. Go medium-fast and stay on your toes. Try for two miles a day.

Blocking practice

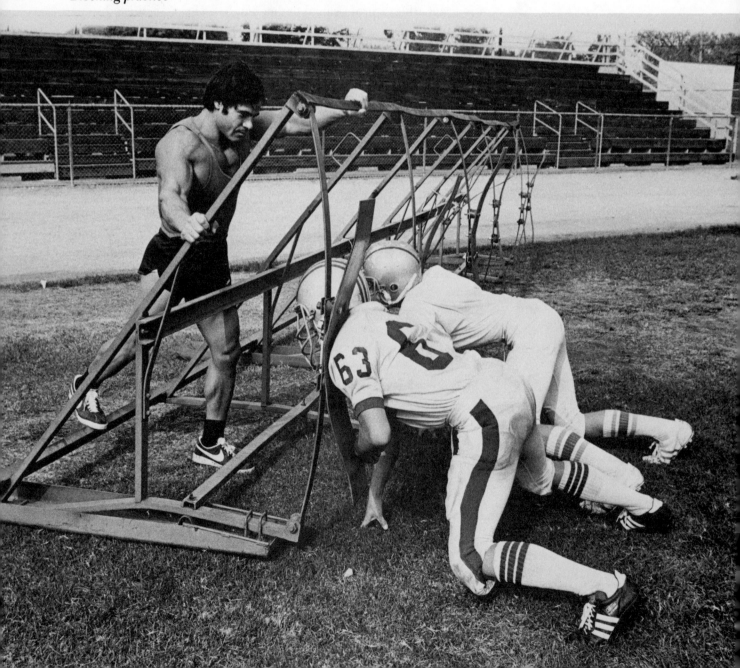

KARATE

1.	Chins	3 sets of 10 reps
2.	Incline Bench Press	3 sets of 12 reps
3.	Lateral Raises	3 sets of 10 reps
4.	Triceps Pushdowns	4 sets of 12 reps
5.	Wrist Curls	3 sets of 10 reps
6.	Reversed Wrist Curls	3 sets of 10 reps
7.	Lunges	3 sets of 20 reps

Place a barbell on your shoulders and step forward vigorously. Step back. Repeat. This exercise will increase your endurance and give tremendous spring to your legs.

8.	Leg Extensions	4 sets of 10 reps
9.	Calf Raises	4 sets of 25 reps
10.	Sit-Ups	4 sets of 30 reps
11.	Leg Raises	4 sets of 30 reps

SOCCER

1.	Calf Raises	5 sets of 20 reps
2.	Leg Raises	4 sets of 25 reps
3.	Squat	4 sets of 20 reps
4.	Chins	4 sets of 10 reps
5.	Lateral Raises	4 sets of 15 reps
6.	Side Bends	3 sets of 25 reps
7.	Sit-Ups	3 sets of 25 reps

Karate

Soccer

BOXING

Note: Use a medium weight for all the exercises in this program.

1. Bench Press	3 sets of 25 reps
2. Incline Bench Press	3 sets of 25 reps
3. Upright Rowing	2 sets of 25 reps
4. Bent-Over Lateral Raises	3 sets of 15 reps
5. Lateral Raises	3 sets of 25 reps
6. Lying Triceps Press	4 sets of 25 reps
7. Leg Extension	3 sets of 20 reps
8. Calf Raises	4 sets of 25 reps

ALL SPORTS

Jumping Rope

Jumping rope improves coordination, agility, speed, cardiovascular strength, and is excellent for the legs. I recommend that you jump rope 3 times a week, 5 to 10 minutes each time. Remember to jump on your toes—not your heels—to avoid compression problems in your spine.

Running

Running is an excellent all-around exercise. You should run with good speed, three times per week, from 1 to 3 miles each time.

I recommend running rather than jogging for many reasons. First of all, it takes less time and is not as boring. But more important, it speeds up the metabolism more than jogging does, which helps in achieving muscle definition. It is also better for the lumbar (lower back) region of the spine. The muscles in that area are more flexed when you run and less likely to be jolted. Jolts cause compression in the lower back. This puts pressure on the nerves that serve the leg muscles and over a period of time weakens the musculature in the legs.

Running

**BECOME THE
OUTSTANDING
COMPETITOR**

In other chapters I have gone into some detail about the importance of mental attitude when you are preparing for athletic events. But there is no way that the subject could be properly covered—even if every chapter were about the same thing. I repeat: The right attitude is absolutely essential. It is the "extra something" that makes you a winner. Without it, though your potential is as great, you will always be mediocre.

One of the most personal forms of competition is arm wrestling. You may have seen some matches on television. I myself have seen many wrestlers prepare, because arm wrestling is often part of the program in bodybuilding contests. The intensity of their mental preparation is almost incredible.

One year, a rather brash young man came to the contest just before the finalists were to go on stage. He had missed the eliminations held earlier in the day. The rules specifically stated that you could not compete in the finals unless you had worked your way through the eliminations. But this young man thought he could take a short-

cut. When he was told that he could not, he was furious. He stomped up and down and challenged all the competitors to wrestle him. The director of the arm wrestling told them they could not accept. The young man continued to stomp around and hurl challenges. He called the competitors every name in the book—from "coward" on down.

The following year, the man who had won the competition arrived at the auditorium ready to do battle again. The first thing he asked was whether the "stomper" of the year before was entered. He was assured that he was.

"Good," said the champion. "I've been waiting all year to get hold of him. I don't care whether or not I win the title again, just as long as I can get hold of that guy's arm."

As luck would have it, both men excelled in the eliminations. The final match was to be between the two of them, before a screaming full house. The champion was calm. In fact, he was a block of ice. He looked at his adversary with contempt. In his mind he had already beaten him. And he was right. I don't think a gorilla could have put the champion's arm down that night. As soon as the signal was given, the knuckles of the brash young man smacked the table and it was over.

The point I want to make is that the champion had fixed his goal upon something very specific. His focus was direct. His concentration was complete. And so was his confidence. This kind of attitude has helped many an athlete become a champion. They played to win. And they did win.

I remember reading about the way Parry O'Brien, the great former Olympic and world shot-put champion, prepared for an important event. His world record in the shot had been broken a few months earlier. He was determined to win it back. To prepare himself, he got a photograph of the man who had broken his record. Then he marked off the exact distance of the new record, and placed the photo at that spot. He practiced by aiming for the picture. He won his record back.

I'm always distressed to hear an athlete say, "Well, I'm sure going to try to win," or "I'm going to do my best." Baloney. I never enter a contest to lose or just "do my best." I never enter a contest with anything in mind but the belief that I will win. And neither should you.

9 Special Problems and What to Do About Them

POSTURE

No one, certainly no athlete, can afford to have sloppy posture. Over a period of time, poor posture can cause serious spinal problems. Examine your posture now. If you have any problems, or see any beginning, the exercises which follow will help you to correct them.

You can check your body alignment by looking at yourself in a full-length mirror and comparing the two sides of your body. You will have to hold a hand mirror in order to see your back.

Begin by looking at your head. Does it tilt to one side? Next check your shoulders. Is one lower or higher than the other? Look at your rib cage. Are your abs pulling to one side? Turn around and look at your spine. Is it straight or does it curve to one side or the other? Are your scapulae level or is one pulled up? Now look sideways and check to see if your head and shoulders are too far forward or too far backward.

In postural problems, there is an imbalance in the musculature. One side is in spasm and the antagonistic (opposite) muscle is weak. Therefore you have to try to stretch the muscles that are in spasm. After you have decided what areas have to be corrected, find the corresponding exercises from those listed below and begin doing them. Do the same number of sets and reps for each side of the body.

HEAD

1. Neck Bends	3 sets of 15 reps

Bend the neck toward the shoulder on each side while trying to touch the shoulder.

SHOULDERS

1. Standing Lateral Raises	3 sets of 15 reps

UPPER BACK

1. Bent-Over Lateral Raises	4 sets of 15 reps
2. Chin-Ups	4 sets of 10 reps

CHEST AND TRICEPS

1. Push-Ups	3 sets of 15 reps
2. Pullovers	3 sets of 15 reps

WAIST AND LOWER BACK

1. Hyperextension	3 sets of 15 reps
2. Standing Side Bends	3 sets of 20 reps
3. Standing Side Leg Raises	2 sets of 15 reps

After your workout, hang from the chinning bar for 5 minutes. You will have to work up to this amount of time. This exercise is excellent because you traction your spine with your own body weight, and all the muscles and ligaments get stretched out.

INJURIES

Muscle Soreness

Muscle soreness is caused by training. Usually, you can differentiate between muscle soreness and an injury by the intensity of the pain. Muscle soreness often begins the day after training and lasts for 3 to 5 days. Pain from an injury begins immediately and can last

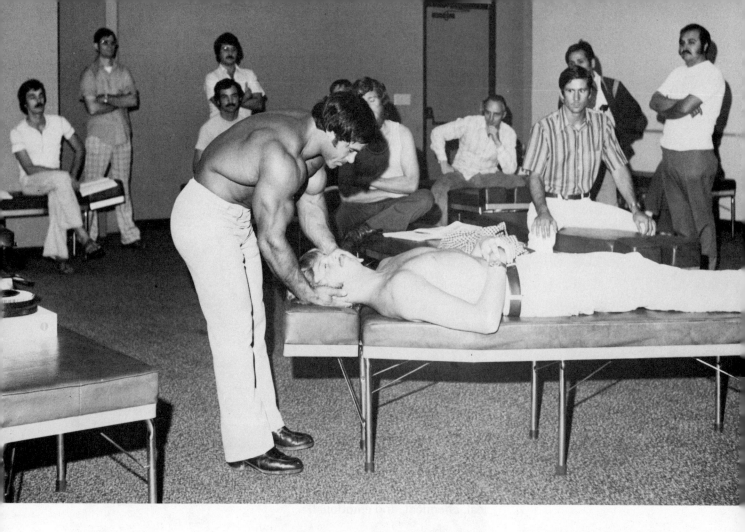

indefinitely. Muscle soreness is generalized throughout the body or body parts that were trained. Pain from an injury is more localized.

I have found that Vitamin C, taken in large doses (1,000 mg) 5 or 6 times a day, helps do away with muscle soreness. As the pain decreases, decrease the amount of Vitamin C. Moist heat (such as from a Jacuzzi, hot shower or hot bath) helps, too.

Muscle soreness is unpleasant, but it's a good sign. It tells you that your muscles have worked hard, and that means that the training session was a successful one. If you continue to train properly, the soreness that results will lessen because the muscles will build up resistance to the exercise.

Muscle Cramps

Muscle cramps are painful muscular contractions. They come and go rapidly. Every athlete has them at one time or another. If you experience cramps on rare occasions, there is no need to be concerned. However, if you have cramps frequently, something is wrong.

One common cause of cramping is poor diet, particularly the

"crash diet" program—high in protein and low in everything else—that bodybuilders often go in for. What they don't realize is that protein intake must be balanced by calcium intake, because the body excretes protein and calcium together. If you take in large amounts of protein, your body will excrete large amounts of protein—and large amounts of calcium along with it. If you haven't upped your calcium intake too, you will develop a calcium deficiency. Then your muscles will begin to cramp.

I do not recommend crash dieting. I do recommend a well-balanced, natural diet with some vitamin and mineral supplements. However, if you do decide on a crash diet, be sure to increase your calcium intake along with your protein intake. Try to take calcium in a liquid or capsule form rather than in tablets. It is easier for the body to assimilate that way.

Muscle Spasm

A spasm, like a cramp, is an involuntary contraction of a muscle. And, like cramps, every athlete has them from time to time. Spasms usually are not as severe as cramps, but they last longer and sometimes become chronic. The muscle shortens (contracts) and stays short. This contraction causes the muscle to weaken. There are numerous reasons why muscle spasms occur, reasons that are physical, chemical, and emotional.

In weight training the most common cause of spasms is improper lifting. The weight, through carelessness or ignorance, is not even,

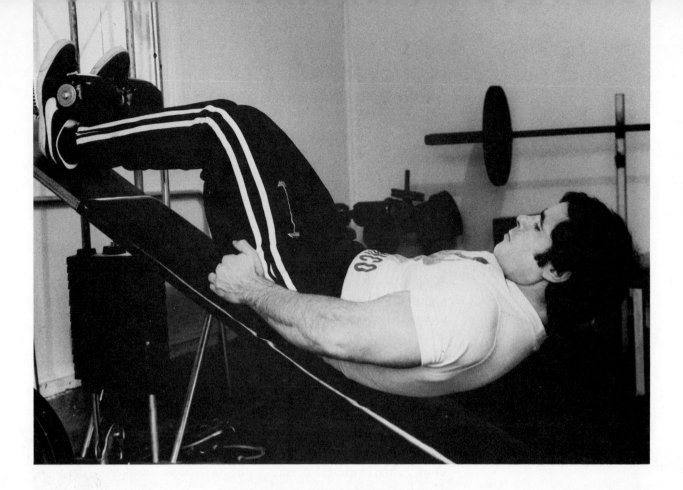

and one side is heavier than the other. You lift it, unaware of the imbalance, and a spasm results. One exercise in which this commonly happens is the press behind the neck. If you press upward with a barbell, and the weight on it is not evenly distributed, you will get a spasm of the upper trapezius on the side where the weight is heavier. (The extra weight pulls the vertebrae in your neck out of alignment, which causes nerve-root compression. So, never exercise without checking the balance on the weights you are using; never train with heavier weights than you can comfortably handle, and never train without warming up thoroughly.

Good nutrition is very important here, just as it is with respect to muscle cramps. A calcium deficiency can result in spasms, too.

Sometimes the cause of a spasm is emotional. I have already said that if you want to become a champion, you must enter the gym with your mind clear. I repeat: Solve your problems—or at least work on them—somewhere else. Tension causes the musculature to contract. Spasms can result. That is one reason why athletes are more prone to injury before a competition. They are tense and keyed up, and that affects their bodies as much as any purely physical problem does. It is true that training helps to reduce tension, but you also have to discipline your mind not to think of anything but the lifts when you are working out.

There are several things you can do at home to get relief from a muscle spasm. First, try to find the center of the spasm. Apply pressure to it. Begin with light pressure and gradually increase it. This should help the muscle to "let go" and relax. Do not use force and do not massage the muscle continuously. Too much muscle stimulation could aggravate the problem. You may also apply moist heat to the area in spasm. Never use a dry heating pad. Use a moist heating pad, a Hydrocollator, a hot water bottle, or take a hot bath, shower, Jacuzzi, etc.

If you have just injured yourself and you notice the muscle beginning to spasm, apply an ice cube directly to the surface of the skin. Keep circulating the ice cube over the area of pain for about 5 to 7 minutes. This procedure may be repeated several times during the day.

If these techniques do not solve the problem, you should seek professional help. Of course, I recommend a doctor of chiropractic.

Strain or Sprain?

Unfortunately, many athletes do not know the difference between these two types of injuries. But it is crucial. A strain involves mus-

cles, tendons, or their attachments; a sprain involves ligaments. A sprain is more severe than a strain and usually takes longer to heal.

STRAINS. Strains result from overuse or overstress of the muscles, tendons or attachments. Both are common in weight training. But they can be avoided if you follow these simple rules.

1. Never overtrain. If your muscles become weak and fatigued, the result may be a strain.
2. When you are tired, leave the gym. Most injuries—including strains—occur on the last set.
3. Warm up properly before you begin to exercise.
4. Avoid all sugar. It is the worst substance there is for muscles. It makes them weak. It raises the blood sugar level very quickly (which is why people think it gives them "quick energy"). But right after it raises it, it causes that level to drop lower than it was before.
5. Concentrate. Don't socialize or let your mind wander while you are training.

Home treatment for a muscle strain is the same as for a spasm (above). Don't work the strained area for 3 to 10 days, depending on the severity of the strain.

SPRAINS. A sprain is an injury to a ligament. In severe sprains, ligaments may be completely torn. The signs of sprain are rapid swelling hotness, inability or partial inability to use the sprained part of the body, and skin discoloration or bruising. To treat a sprain, place an ice cube on the surface of the skin. Move it in a circular manner for 5 to 7 minutes until the area is numb. You can also place the entire area in ice-cold water. This will alleviate the pain and prevent further swelling. If the sprain is not severe, mild pressure-point techniques will help. If it is severe, immobilize the area completely. You should also have it x-rayed to rule out the possibility of fracture. It is best to keep the sprained area supported by an ace bandage while training. Use a body support if both the muscles and the ligaments have been weakened.

Bursitis

The bursae are situated around joints and tendons, where they provide protection against pressure and friction. Bursitis is a painful swelling of a bursa. Common forms of bursitis include the shoulder, elbow, knee and ankle.

One of the main causes of bursitis is overactivity of a joint. This happens in bodybuilding when too many exercises involving the

1968—Mr. Italy

same joint—especially the elbow or shoulder joints—are done. Except when you are training, the best treatment is partial immobilization of the joint. When you are training, the joint should be completely immobilized. You must not exercise it at all. Training must be altered to take this into consideration. If the area is overstressed before it has had a chance to heal completely, the symptoms will return.

For home treatment, use moist heat. Hydrocollators and hot water bottles work best because they allow the heat to penetrate deep into the muscles. Apply the heat for 10 to 15 minutes at a time, 2 or 3 times a day, depending on the severity of the pain. Calcification around the joint could develop, so if the pain becomes chronic, you should seek professional help.

Tendonitis and Tenosynovitis

Tendonitis is the inflammation of a tendon. Tenosynovitis is the inflammation of the synovia surrounding the tendon. Both are

107

1969—Mr. Europe

usually caused by strain from unaccustomed overuse, but may be due to a direct blow or to an infection. Do not train the affected region with heavy weights. On the other hand, light, full-motion exercises, such as stretching, reaching and bending are beneficial. The same heat treatment we recommend for bursitis will also help.

Fracture

The standard definition of a fracture is a break in the continuity of bone. However, a fracture is really more than a broken bone. It is a rupture of all soft tissue in the injured area. It may be accompanied by extensive soft-tissue swelling, hemorrhaging into muscles and joints, dislocation of joints, rupture of tendons, bruises or sev-

108

erance of nerves, and damage to major blood vessels. A simple fracture is one that occurs without a break in the overlying skin; a compound fracture is one in which the tissue is broken and the bones are exposed.

If you have reason to suspect that you have fractured some part of your body, you must see a doctor immediately. You will need to be examined and x-rayed. Do not attempt to treat fractures yourself.

10 Nutrition

I never cease to wonder about the reasoning of some people. Let anything happen to that hunk of metal called a car, and the owner will almost hock his home to get it well. If the man at the garage tells him that he needs this or that additive to keep the engine in good condition, he'll accept the recommendation as an "order." But tell that same person to supplement his diet with specific nutritional aids to maintain better health and as often as not he'll tell you you're "some kind of health nut." He'll spend a fortune on his car at the slightest sign of a problem, but wait until he's at death's door before he'll do anything about his body. He wouldn't put water or sludge into the gas tank of his car and expect it to run, but he will drink beer, eat pizza and suck on cigarettes and expect to go on forever.

I can think of no single factor that is of greater importance to a person's health than proper nutrition. Without the right "body fuel" all the exercise in the world would be in vain. This doesn't mean that you have to live in a cave on nuts and berries in order to be

1970—Mr. Universe

1971—Mr. World

healthy. But it does mean that you need something other than cola and hot dogs. Before considering specific food groups and menus, I think it would be a good idea for you to understand the basic elements you're working with.

VITAMINS

Vitamins are organic substances, essential to nutrition. They regulate metabolic processes, help to provide energy from the foods we eat, repair body cells and tissue, and promote growth.

Vitamin	Function
A	promotes healthy skin, hair and eyes
B1 (thiamine)	aids carbohydrate metabolism, digestion
B2 (riboflavin)	aids digestion, vision, iron absorption
B3 (niacin)	aids nervous and digestive systems; improves circulation
B6 (pyridoxine)	aids nervous and digestive systems; protects body from infections
B12	aids nervous and digestive systems; aids in blood formation
Biotin (a B-complex vitamin)	aids digestion, utilization of B12, folic acid and pantothenic acid
Choline (a B-complex vitamin)	aids digestion of fats, essential for health of liver and kidneys; protects nerves
Folic Acid (a B-complex vitamin)	aids in red blood cell formation, protein metabolism
Inositol (a B-complex vitamin)	necessary in lecithin formation, fat metabolism
PABA (para-aminobenzoic acid, a B-complex vitamin)	aids protein digestion, red blood cell formation; promotes healthy skin
Pantothenic Acid (a B-complex vitamin)	needed for energy, digestion, other vitamin utilization
C (ascorbic acid)	fights infection; maintains strength of blood vessels; aids in healing
D	aids in the absorption of calcium and metabolism of phosphorus; essential for healthy bones and teeth
E	promotes healing; retards scarring; protects red blood cells; strengthens walls of blood vessels

MINERALS

Minerals are inorganic substances. They are essential for the formation of bones and muscles, and for the healthy functioning of every organ in your body. (If you lack minerals, all the vitamins in the world are useless. Vitamins can't work without them.)

112

1975—Mr. Olympia

Minerals	Function
Calcium	aids in blood clotting, muscle growth and contraction, normal heart function, nerve transmission; builds and maintains healthy bones and teeth
Chromium	aids in regulation of blood sugar
Copper	aids in the formation of red blood cells
Iodine	aids in functioning of thyroid gland, regulation of energy; promotes healthy skin and teeth
Iron	gives vitality and builds red blood cells
Magnesium	necessary for the proper use of proteins and carbohydrates, proper functioning of muscles and nerves; aids complexion; promotes healthy sleep
Manganese	activates other minerals; aids in proper nutrition and fertility
Phosphorus	nourishes brain; promotes proper growth of bones and teeth, proper function of nervous system and kidneys

PROTEINS

Proteins are the fundamental structural components of all living cells. They are the body's building blocks. The word *protein* itself comes from the Greek and means "of first importance."

Proteins are made up of molecules called amino acids. There are twenty-two amino acids found in the body; thirteen can be made by the body itself. But we have to get the other nine from the foods we eat. These nine are called the "essential" amino acids, and foods which contain them are called "complete" proteins.

Exercising, as you know, temporarily breaks down body tissue. It is rebuilt—stronger than ever—during rest. The elements needed to do this building job are the complete proteins. You can see how essential it is that you get enough of them.

Here is a list of the essential amino acids. If you supplement your diet with a protein product, make sure the label on the package lists them. Natural foods containing complete proteins are milk, soy bean, egg, cheese, poultry, fish, and meat.

Histidine	Isoleucine
Lysine	Threonine
Tryptophan	Methionine
Phenylalanine	Valine
Leucine	

114

1976—Mr. Olympia

CARBOHYDRATES

Carbohydrates are the simple sugars or substances formed by simple sugars. They are the heat and energy producers, the "fuel" foods.

Carbohydrates aid in the metabolism of fats. They help to maintain the functional integrity of the nervous system and are a source of energy for the brain. They are essential, then, but you must establish a proper balance of exercise and carbohydrate intake. If you take in more carbohydrates than the body uses, they will end up as fatty deposits.

Carbohydrates are found chiefly in grains, vegetables, fruits, syrups and sugars.

FATS

Fats serve as a concentrated source of heat and energy. They are essential for normal tissue function. Foods rich in fatty acids are butter, oils and nuts. As with carbohydrates, a balance between need and supply should be established.

Now that you know something about the basic elements of nutrition, it's time to start thinking about—and perhaps changing—your own eating habits. The best advice I can give you is to keep your diet as natural and as simple as possible. Try to eliminate all processed and refined foods. They are usually full of hidden calories and have very little nutritional value. Also, try to eliminate all *sugar*, *fat* and *salt*. We take in more of these substances than we realize, for they are hidden in many of our foods. Your body does need some natural carbohydrates, some fat and some salt, but unless you are careful, you take in much more than you need or can use.

There are many different opinions about protein and what kind of protein is best for athletes. In my opinion, the best protein is from natural foods such as eggs, fish, dairy products, poultry and meat. These foods are easily digested and absorbed by the body. Synthetic protein often is not. Also, most synthetic protein products contain sugar and chemicals.

Remember, the body requires protein, carbohydrates, and fat for its normal functioning, so be sure to include foods that contain all three in your daily diet. Below are some of my specific recommendations about the foods you should eat.

BREAD. Try to get bread that is coarse and heavy such as seven-grain, stone-ground. This type of bread is high in nutrition and roughage.

CEREALS. Use the seven-grain granola cereals. They are high in minerals and B vitamins and are excellent sources of bulk and roughage.

116

RAW SEEDS AND NUTS.   In their natural form—not roasted—seeds and nuts are great for snacking and very nutritious. They are especially high in trace minerals, the B-complex vitamins, and natural oil. However, they are also high in calories, so if you have a tendency to be heavy, be careful not to overeat.

OILS AND FATS.   Use only small amounts of pure vegetable oil. (The only oil I use is olive oil.) Eliminate all fried food, mayonnaise, margarine and oily dressings.

FRUITS AND VEGETABLES.   These foods should be eaten abundantly every day. (I have at least three different kinds of fruit and two large raw vegetable salads daily. I also eat steamed vegetables with lunch and dinner.)

CHEESE. Cheese is an excellent food, but it does contain much fat. Read labels carefully, and try to select low-fat or skim-milk cheese. Stay away from cheeses that contain preservatives, and those that are processed and come in tubes, jars, or cans.

MILK. Milk is an excellent source of protein. You can drink it straight or use it for making yogurt. (I do, and I eat it daily.)

EGGS. Eggs are among the most nutritious foods on earth, but they are relatively high in fats and cholesterol. (I use fertile eggs and eat two or three daily.)

FOWL. Try to get chicken or turkey that is grown without hormones or chemicals. Remove the skin, which is very high in fat, before you bake it.

SEA FOODS. Sea food is generally low in fat, high in protein and the essential amino acids, and high in trace minerals. It is also low in calories. Fresh fish is best. It should be baked or broiled. If you use canned fish, use only the water-packed kind.

MEATS. Try to get meat that does not contain hormones or chemicals. Cut off all the fat. (Even then, it will still be 10% to 15% fat.) Eliminate all meats which have a high fat content, such as bacon, sausages, hamburger, luncheon meats, weiners, etc. Meat should be broiled or baked or roasted in the oven.

If you eat the kinds of foods mentioned above, your body will respond to weight-training exercises much more quickly. You will look better and feel better, and you will become stronger almost at once. So eat properly and carefully, and train yourself to eliminate food-less food—ice cream, candy, alcohol, etc.—from your diet entirely. As I have often said, before you put anything into your mouth, ask yourself what that particular food will do for your body.

Here is the diet that I follow myself. It is balanced to meet the needs of people in heavy training.

Breakfast

3 fresh eggs
1 fresh fruit in season, or a large glass of fresh-squeezed orange juice
A small dish of homemade plain yogurt (made with raw milk), with granola cereal
A glass of mineral water, with vitamin and mineral supplements

119

Lunch

A large fresh vegetable salad, with a small amount of oil-and-vinegar dressing

1 cooked fresh vegetable (never frozen or canned)

A large portion of fresh broiled protein, such as fish, chicken, or prime cuts of beef, lamb, or liver

A large glass of mineral water

Mid-afternoon

A plate of selected cheeses, with fresh fruit in season

Dinner

Similar to lunch

Later in the Evening

A small dish of fresh yogurt

I attribute a great deal of the muscle and power I now possess to the foundation established by sound nutrition I received early in life. Our foods were entirely natural, uncontaminated by additives, hormones or chemicals of any kind. Unfortunately, we in America are "blessed" with the "benefits" of modern farming and food processing. By the time it reaches us, most of our food has been boiled, dehydrated, and poisoned. That is why supplementary vitamins and minerals are often needed. Remember, optimum function requires optimum nutrition.

11 Roundtable

A great deal of my time is spent traveling around the country lecturing and giving demonstrations before the student bodies of colleges and high schools. Quite often, after I've finished my talk, a number of students approach me with questions. Some are asked so frequently that I felt you might be wondering about the same ones too. Imagine then, if you will, that you're sitting in the bleachers of the local high school football field throwing questions to me. I hope I give you some helpful answers.

Q. How fast should I do the reps of each set?

A. That depends on what you want to get from the exercise. When reps are done rapidly they tend to give a quicker pump, but less weight can usually be used. This will act to break down tissue. In your exercising for abdominal definition, fast reps are a good

121

idea; if you wish to pack on muscular size and power in a chest exercise, slower reps are better. Determine carefully what you want to get from the exercise before you start doing it.

Q. I've always had a hard time getting a good pump. Is there something I'm doing wrong?

A. It could be that you're overtraining. When we first start we sometimes get so enthusiastic that we tend to do too much. Cut down on some of the sets and reps, change the weight and vary your exercises. Remember, they affect different people in different ways. You may get a good pump from one exercise. Your friend may get a good pump from another. You must train instinctively. Remember, too, that a pump isn't necessarily the most important thing in your workout. I've seen men who train for nothing but a pump in their programs. As a result they have little more than bloated tissue that disappears with the first layoff. You want muscle that lasts. That kind only comes when it is based upon a foundation of power.

Q. How important is heavy training? Shouldn't I also train for definition?

A. I can't stress this often enough. Stand in front of a mirror. What do you see? What do your training partners see? What do you need? Once you decide the answers to those questions you can develop a program that will give you the results you want. Less weight and higher reps will give you definition. Larger weights and less reps will tend to add size and power. To me, the most important thing is to be as strong as you look. I can always tell when a phony is posing. A man who trains for strength looks that way. There is an undefinable quality in the man who has strength as opposed to the bloated lightweight. If you want an 18-inch arm be sure that it has 18 inches of power behind it.

Q. How much training should I do on the day of the contest?

A. None. In fact, I don't think you should train for the last two days before the competition. If you've trained properly, your body will benefit from the rest. Your muscles will pump a lot faster and better, however, if you pump just before your appearance. Just give yourself at least five minutes of rest before you go on to compete. There's nothing more disconcerting than watching someone pose while he's struggling to catch his breath. Also, if you're too bloated from a pump, you'll tend to lose some of your muscular separation.

Q. Whenever I shave my body before a physique contest I seem to break out in a rash. What am I doing wrong?

A. You might have naturally sensitive skin. Frequent applications of Vitamin E cream may help. Shave two days before a contest and that should also help. A final hint is to shave in the direction of the hair growth, never against it.

Q. Should I use steroids?

A. No. Steroids came into prominence after the Second World War as a substance that would accelerate tissue regrowth and repair in war wounds. They served a worthwhile purpose. One day, some bodybuilders discovered that by taking steroids their bodybuilding gains would come faster and they would become stronger. What they didn't figure on were the adverse side effects or runaway tissue growth. Recently a well-known bodybuilder wrote an article claiming that he had used steroids for years without any ill effects. I just heard that he was admitted to the hospital because of his use of steroids. And I've heard of many people who became psychologically dependent on them. Who needs it? Build honest muscle. It shows and it's safe.

I hope I've answered some of your questions. I know there must be many more that I haven't even touched upon. Maybe someday you'll be in the audience—and I'll be able to answer your questions in person.

12 Some Final Thoughts

This book is finished. But is it? Will advice on the subject ever be finished? I don't think so. There will always be something more to say. Something that wasn't thought of before. Something new.

I have tried to inspire you as well as instruct you. I've tried to help you find in yourself the special quality that makes a person a champion. I hope I've succeeded. I hope too that I have helped you understand the importance of balancing your life. No matter how successful you become in athletics, don't neglect your mental power. And don't be modest. You have it—the very act of concentrating on and achieving a physical goal demonstrates the power of your mind. Use that power to better yourself in your studies. Many of the body-builders I've known have been professional people—chiropractic doctors, teachers, physicists, and corporate executives. They know, I know, and you should know, that an inch more of muscle doesn't mean a pound less of brains. It never has.

I hesitate to say goodbye. It's like leaving a friend that you know you may never see again. There are so many things you want to say, things you may have forgotten, things that should have been said differently, areas that should have been emphasized more or em-phasized less. If, however, this book helps you to achieve your physical and mental goals, then I leave with a sense of fulfillment and satisfaction.